The School Pianist

Iris Broughton

Iris Broughton and Michael Parkinson

© Iris Broughton and Michael Parkinson 2025

The rights of Iris Broughton and Michael Parkinson to be identified as the authors of this work have been asserted by them in accordance with sections 77 and 78 of the Copyright, Designs and Patents Act 1988.
All rights reserved. No part of this book may be reprinted or reproduced or utilised in any form or by any electronic, mechanical, or other means, now known or hereafter invented, including photocopying and recording, or in any information storage or retrieval system, without the prior written consent of the authors, the authors' representatives or a licence permitting copying in the UK issued by the Copyright Licensing Agency Ltd.
www.cla.co.uk

ISBN 978-1-78792-085-9

Book design, layout and production management by Into Print

www.intoprint.net

+44 (0)1604 832149

Front cover photograph:

Seven year old Mandy Giles made a presentation to me in 1977. The concert celebrated one hundred years since the opening of Haydn Primary School at Sherwood, Nottingham

Contents

	Acknowledgements	4
	Introduction by Michael Parkinson	5
1	Early years	7
2	Work and Weddings	14
3	My Dream Job	16
4	Resuming my Career	23
5	Retirement	33
6	My Mother and Father, Iris and Dennis	40
7	My Aunty Iris	45
8	My Cousin – Iris Broughton	48
9	My Music Collection	52
10	My Tribute to Iris	57
	By the same author	60

Acknowledgements

I thank my wife, Joan, for the help she has given, the chapter that she has provided and her opinions on which pictures to use.

Mrs Jenny Green who has edited every chapter as she has in all my books and I am very grateful for her contribution.

Thank you to Neil Broughton and Paul Parker for the chapters they have submitted.

The Editor of the Nottingham Post newspaper for giving me permission to use information and cuttings from what was originally called the Nottingham Evening Post.

A huge thank you to Iris Broughton who has patiently tried to answer the questions I have asked. She has had to endure me constantly remarking 'Yes, I've got all that' and I have never complained about her saying 'I can't remember'.

Thank you to Anne and Mark Webb of Paragon Publishing for helping to make Iris's dream come true.

Introduction

by Michael Parkinson (Curator)

Iris Broughton is a cousin of my wife Joan but we have always referred to her as Aunty Iris. I have been close to her because of our mutual interest in music and she usually attended concerts that I promoted.

In July 2024, when Iris was 96 years of age Joan and I took her to Mapperley Golf Club which is close to her house and enjoyed a lunch as we did periodically. Iris told me that she wanted to ask me something important when we got back to her home but refused to tell us what it was about. When we were back at her house she showed me some sheets of foolscap lined paper with handwritten writing and told me that this was her story. She was aware that I had written and published books and asked me to help her achieve her aim. I told her that I was in the process of writing a book and would not be able to look at her project until September, at the earliest.

It was the middle of October 2024 when I looked at the story and I realised it was a daunting task because the thirteen pages of text only included a disjointed introduction and no story. The opening line was 'It's August 1st 2014 and at the ripe old age of 86, I'm trying to write about the story of my life and loved ones'. On the final page, number thirteen, she had written these words. 'Now at 93 reading the words I've written I know I need help because I have repeated myself many times. I would like someone to sort this out for me, some time'.

When I read the words that Iris had written when she was 93. I felt very emotional because she had asked me to achieve her ambition and I decided to do it somehow. It was now 2024 so it was three years since Iris had written that plea for help and ten years since she had started her project.

The obstacle that I had to overcome was that Iris was nearly deaf and her sight was deteriorating. I am a loud mouth so was able to converse with her and decided to use a technique of videoing my conversations and using the resulting video, later at home, to put her story into words. I had made a list of questions and the first video session resulted in nearly two hours of video. The next session took a further 1 hour 30 minutes and we did a further two recording sessions.

The School Pianist – Iris Broughton

> Its August 1st 2014 and at the ripe old age at 86, I'm trying to write the story of my life and loved ones I believe everyone has a tale to tell My name is IRIS BROUGHTON PARKER and nee PARKER I was born 8-2-1928 at No 1, ST. MARKS STREET, which is just off HUNTINGDON St. near to the VICTORIA RAILWAY STATION

First attempt, age 86

> Now at 93 reading the words I've written I know I NEED HELP because I have repeated myself many time. I would like someone to sort this out for me. Sometime.

Plea for help, age 93

Chapter 1

Early Years

At the ripe old age of 96 years I have decided to write the story of my life and loved ones, I believe that everyone has a tale to tell. I was born on 8 February 1928 at number 1 St Marks Street in Nottingham. This is just off Huntingdon Street, near to the Victoria Railway Station (now demolished). My parents were Catherine and Herbert Parker who were married in October 1920. I had a wonderful brother, Wallace who was six years my senior, he was born in 1922.

My father, Herbert Parker was born in 1894 and left school at the age of twelve so was just twenty when the 'Great War' started on 28 July 1914. He volunteered to fight for England the following month, August, having no work at the time he enlisted. At first he was in the Robin Hoods and was sent to France, he was later transferred to the Cheshire Regiment and was sent to Gallipoli where he fought alongside Australian troops. He spent the rest of his war there, often being behind the lines with dysentery, malaria and double pneumonia. He was a Corporal, Acting Sergeant and came home a very sick man. After some time recuperating he worked on the railway for a while but later, became a Billposter, working for 'Mills and Rockley', and pushed a wheelbarrow. He later progressed to driving a black electric van with gold lettering. Mother, Catherine Oldham, went to work at thirteen as a sewing machinist and became a blouse designer and after being married she carried on working for a while. Then she did dressmaking at home and made wedding and bridesmaid dresses, anything that people asked for. Mum had a few piano lessons but never progressed very far, as she said, she couldn't earn any money while she was practising. So she gave it up but made sure that Wallace and I both had piano lessons later on. My Dad went to Sycamore School as a young boy and learned how to swim in a cold water pool underneath the building. During the Second World War it was prepared to be used as a mortuary but fortunately it never happened and it was later converted into a library. Wallace, my brother, was also born at 1 St Marks Street. He joined the church choir at St Marks on Huntingdon Street when he was about four years old. He was the soloist there until his voice broke. I had

The School Pianist – Iris Broughton

Scarlet Fever or Diphtheria, I just can't remember which, but I do know I was sent into an isolation hospital where whatever parents brought me had to be left behind. They could see you only through the windows.

At five years of age I went to St Marks Infant School, just round the corner from where we lived. One day, when I was about nine, I was walking to the library along Shakespeare Street when I was knocked down by a van and ended up in the Nottingham General Hospital for two weeks, with concussion and bruises. This caused me to have migraines which continued for many years. My mother went to see someone and obtained a sum of money because the clothes I was wearing were all torn and blood stained.

My mothers mother Sarah Ann Eliza Oldham lived with us for the remainder of her life after she became a widow at the age of 39. Her husband, George Oldham, died of a heart attack aged 42 in 1917. He was crossing a field to get the train from South Normanton, coming home to Nottingham, and had over one hundred and twenty-seven pounds in his pocket when he died. He had a green-grocery business and could neither read or write but left nearly five hundred and eighty pounds in his will.

In 1934 Mum and Dad bought 45 Shelton Street for the grand sum of £350, it had not got a bathroom so, before we took possession, one was fitted. We had always had one at 1 St Marks Street. Grandma Oldham still lived with us (I loved her, as we grew older I shared all my secrets with her) we shared a bedroom with twin beds.

Wallace and I both went to St Marks Sunday School on Huntingdon Street. We both had piano lessons with Miss Edith Walker of 40 Robin Hood Chase. Wallace began at age ten until fourteen. I started at age seven and continued until I got my degree with the Victoria College of Music, London on 26 July 1949. This was founded in 1890 with registered number 16898. The piano teacher's house was demolished after the war and we lost contact with each other after many years of friendship. Miss Walker and I, on Sundays, used to play piano duets on two pianos. She played the beautiful grand piano and myself the upright.

I had been singing and playing at Church socials and, during the war at teas. Miss Walker, my music teacher, accompanied me when I sang. I left Sycamore school, aged 14, and started work in the Jack Brentnall music shop and met Joy Smith who is still a friend after all these years. I did not stay there very long as the manageress Miss Smith (no relation to Joy) wanted us to spend Sundays with her at her abode at Kegworth to socialise and to play piano in the local pubs in

Early Years

the evening. Neither Joy nor I wanted to spend our only free day with her so we both left. I then went to work in a factory to learn how to make ladies underwear, I worked there for three years at Gordon and Gordon on North Sherwood Street. Mr Gordon Thorpe, the owner was the organist at the Albert Hall for the Nottingham Harmonic Choir. Mr and Mrs Roberts, the manager and manageress lived in West Bridgford and one evening asked me to play at a musical evening at their house. The time flew and the buses stopped at 9 o'clock, during the war so I had to walk all the way home to Shelton Street. (A good thing it was summer with light nights and double summertime). I was looking very smart as always because my mother made all my clothes, I remember I was wearing a dusky pink dress, a long fawn coat, dark brown shoes, hat and gloves and carrying my music case. A car stopped as I was walking over Trent Bridge, a man asked me if I would like a lift, he was a business man on his way to the Post Office on Huntingdon Street. After he had posted his letters, he took me to Woodborough Road and asked if he could see me again but didn't make further arrangements. I was seventeen and so naive (but how lucky for the man to be a GENTLEMAN). I thanked my lucky stars and never accepted any lifts again.

At 15 I went to Sunday School and played piano each week at Holy Trinity Church in Trinity Square. During the war the Vicar at our Church, Revd Harry Holden, who later officiated at my wedding, began working for the Red Cross, so many of our prisoners were getting parcels. I collected one from Shelton Street every Sunday morning. The Holy Trinity Church Hall on Colville Street had a lovely stage and back rooms for changing clothes, there was a kitchen where we made sandwiches, tea and biscuits. We entertained the parish with several plays and musical evenings. We also had a sale of work for which our mothers made pickle onions and other things which they put into jars to sell. One evening, while playing badminton, I found my doctor was in the other team. He said he never thought he would ever play against one of 'his babies', Dr Roy Carlson had cared for my mother when I was born. He was a lovely man and in those days there were only a few cars on the road, if he was passing he would always toot his horn. That would have been when I was about twenty. By coincidence, another member of the Colson family, was a surgeon who treated warts that I had around my thumb nail.

We were given collecting tins at the Church Hall and once a month we had them emptied. Mum and I went collecting the first Sunday of the month, just collecting on Shelton Street. Afterwards, I did it from age 11 to 17 and once stood in the foyer at the Ritz cinema with a tin, my friend Sylvia helped as well.

The School Pianist – Iris Broughton

It was so good to hear from mothers, who had sons who were prisoners, and were receiving parcels, it was worth collecting every Sunday morning during the war. That was my war effort plus entertaining the troops in a big house on Robin Hood Chase, Mother was always there, making teas for the forces. I joined a Youth Club at the age of fourteen in St Marks Church Hall on Huntingdon Street. It is now Wrights, a business for artists, selling paints etcetera. We did some plays to entertain the local public, then at 17 we went into the Trinity Church new Church Hall on Colville Street and played badminton, darts and table tennis. Sylvia and I were in charge of the canteen which involved coupons for bread and other things. The curate, Revd John Thomas Drinkall gave us the jobs. The Youth Club belonging to Holy Trinity Church admitted people between the ages of 15 to 25. We had some very good times together. Once a year the Church did a 'Bring and Buy' sale. One evening (this must have been after the war) we put on three plays. At the Youth Club, then 17, I met Ken who was discharged from the war being wounded in the leg in Burma. He became rather interested in me and later when the war was over and Wallace was home from the Navy we went to Blackpool altogether. I realised I didn't want Ken, and made it clear I did not want to see him again.

That's when, in 1948, I met Dennis Broughton, my future husband. He was on demobilisation leave during his National Service, he had been in India for 18 months. Dennis also sang in the Church choir at Wilford and, after the war, later at St Nicholas in Town. The vicar who had a son in the RAF asked Dennis to sing 'Bless This House' at his sons wedding. I went to the Church to hear Dennis sing the solo and was met at the entrance by a lady usher who said are you with the Bride or Groom, I said, 'I am with the choirboy. My brother, Wallis was married to Dorothy in 1950 at St Paul's Church, Hyson Green. In the following year, Dennis and I were married at Holy Trinity Church in Nottingham on 24 March 1951. The Church has now been demolished and there is a car park, shops and offices on the site called Trinity Square.

I've by passed the war years when we were children and not evacuated. We lived near the Victoria Railway Station which was a target for the bombers but were very lucky because bombs dropped to the East or West but missed us. Nottingham is built on a labyrinth of rocks where years ago beer was stored in caves and kept at the correct temperatures. Some caves were used as shelters during the war. We went to one of these at first, through an entrance on Mansfield Road, but it was so cold that, afterwards, we went, under the stairs at home, when the sirens blew.

Early Years

Left to right Lavinia Oldham, Bride Catherine Oldham, Groom, Herbert Parker, Best man Thomas Parker, wedding October 1920

Mum, Catherine with Iris age 8

The School Pianist – Iris Broughton

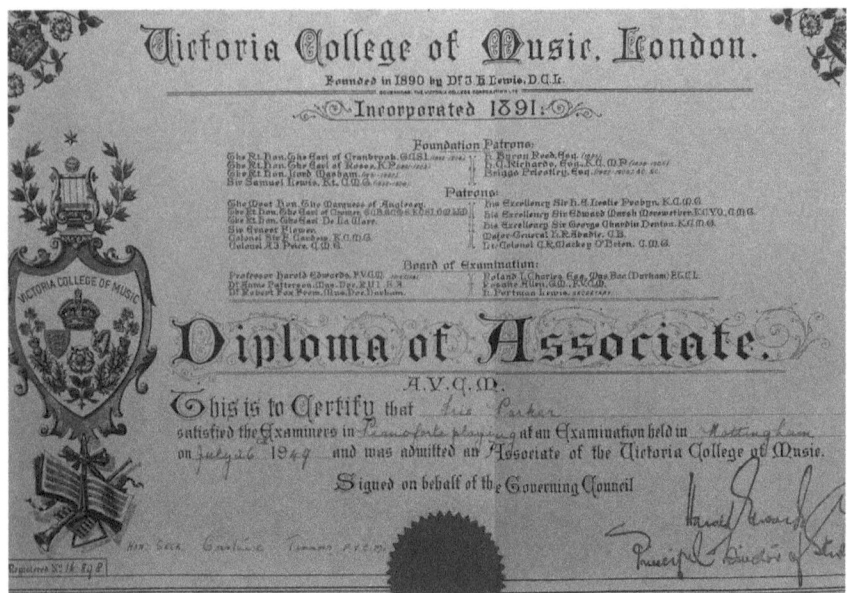

The Diploma awarded to Iris on 26 July 1949

Left to right, Dennis Broughton, Groom Wallis Parker Bride Dorothy Welbourne Iris, Bridesmaid, the brides Father

Early Years

Miss Edith Walker, my music teacher and close friend

Back, Me and Edith, front, Mum. Catherine (Betty piano pupil), Dad, Herbert

Chapter 2

Work and Weddings

I finished working at Gordon & Gordon who were underwear manufacturers when I was 17 and went to a company called H Brown on Alfred Street because they made ladies dresses. My Mother thought the experience would be useful for me to become a dress maker, as she was. I did not do that for long and worked in a shoe shop called Stead and Simpson. One day Matt Monro, a singer who was performing at the Theatre Royal that week, came in and bought a cheap pair of Black patent leather shoes which, I was told, he wore on stage. I did various jobs and finished up working in a hairdressing shop and found that my constant piano playing had made my fingers very strong. Because of this I soon became a good hairdresser but did not like doing facials. They wanted me to do facials so I left and went to another shop where they allowed me to just do hairdressing. They told me that I was on a months trial and if I did all right they would take me on and they did.

When Dennis finished his National Service he went to work with his brother-in-law as a welder and they used to do big jobs for different people. But if one of them got a spark in his eye or in a shoe they had to go to hospital and their pay stopped the minute they left the factory even though the accident had happened at work. So later on Dennis asked my brother Wallis, who was a milkman, if he could get him a job on the Co-op. Wallis said 'Of course I can'. So Dennis gave notice to finish at the welding job, which he had done for 13 years, and started work as a delivery roundsman which he did until he retired. When Dennis finished the welding job his brother-in-law told him he would be 'nothing, only a glorified errand boy' and I thought that was terrible. But, 'the glorified errand boy did a lot better than him, because, later on, Dennis and I bought our own house.

Wallis and Dorothy were married in October 1950 at St Pauls Church, Hyson Green and lived in a terraced house on Wellington Street which is just round the corner from St Marks Street, where we lived. Mam and Dad bought the house and when Dennis and I got married on 24 March 1951 we lived with

Work and Weddings

them for about three years. We shared the kitchen and the bathroom and then the house next door became empty so Mam and Dad put a deposit down on that for Dennis and me. After that, my father took ill and my parents bought a caravan near where we live now and when we went there I saw a house for sale and said to Wallis 'I'm going for that' because we had saved up quite a bit of money. So Wallis said 'If you're leaving, I'm leaving' and they bought a house on Bardney Road, just round the corner from us. Their house had central heating and ours didn't so we got central heating installed in ours. Our son, Neil, was born on 7 July 1955.

Wallis and Dorothy wedding October 1950, Iris was the Bridesmaid

Iris and Dennis with bridesmaids Joan and Ann (on left)

Chapter 3

My Dream Job

When I was 32 years of age I was a school dinner lady at The William Booth School on Notintone Street, at Sneinton in Nottingham. There were thirty children and at dinner time with three tables and ten children seated at each table. The Head Teacher supervised the children at one of the tables, the School Secretary at another and me at the third. The tables were nicely set out with tureens for the soup. After they had eaten I had to supervise all the children as they played in the playground. When it was time for them to go back into school I was responsible making sure that they were all clean and tidy. There was a cloakroom where each child had a bag with comb, towel and a flannel so I had to make sure the children used them.

One day as I went back into school I heard someone playing 'Teddy Bears Picnic' on the piano and thought to myself 'If I can't do better than that I'll eat my hat'. I thought I could make use of my piano playing diploma, and had seen a notice on the board, so decided to apply for a job as a school pianist. The Vicar of Holy Trinity Church and my music teacher wrote references for me and after a few days I received a letter asking me to meet a man named Kenneth Eade who was the Head of Music for Nottingham Schools. He asked me some questions, put some music in front of me, and asked me to go to the piano and play it. He immediately told me that I had the job. It was full time Staff position with a wage of £28 a month. I had to sign a paper which said that in addition to working all day on Monday to Friday I had to play wherever the children were singing in the evenings plus Saturday and Sunday, I did not receive any extra money for that. It was later changed to an hourly rate but I can't remember when and if I was better off or not.

My son was six when I started that job so it must have been 1961. The first school that I worked at was Walter Halls Primary School on Wells Road, Mapperley, Nottingham and it is still there today. I was to work there for full days on Monday, Wednesday and Friday every week. The head was Mary Littlewood and I went in to see her on the Friday of the first week and said 'I've come to tell you that I am not staying because I can't do it. She asked me why and

My Dream Job

I replied 'I just can't because every half hour some different man or woman has been coming to me and asking me to play something new and sometimes I can't even find the sheet music, I just can't do it'. I told Mary that I had written a letter to Mr Eade telling him that I could not continue. Mary told me that she could intervene, so she said 'Go to the piano Mrs Broughton and I will send a child for you and when the child arrives I want you to come to my room'. So I went to her room and she left and phoned Kenneth Eade to come. There was a tray of coffee and biscuits while I waited. When Mr Eade came in he said to me, What's your problem Mrs Broughton? I said 'I can't do it' and explained my dilemma, he said 'Of course you can', 'You will find, in years to come, all these youngsters coming from college to teach music will be helped by your knowledge', with that, I kept the job and I stayed for 32 years. I must say that this was an example of how good Miss Littlewood and Mr Eade were at their jobs. I enjoyed my work but on one occasion I did have a problem because a young teacher was telling the pupils something that I knew to be completely wrong and I was trying to explain it to the young lady. The Headmaster overheard and spoke very sharply to me. He said 'She's the teacher, not you'. I thought he was very rude and he was the only headmaster that I did not like in my whole career. He did not ask me and other staff members to do things but barked out orders with no manners. A couple of years after that incident there was a heavy snowfall with about 8 inches of snow on the ground. I went to work at the Seeley School on Perry Road in Sherwood on the Wednesday morning. When I arrived the headmaster told me that he had sent the staff home and closed the school for the day but there were some children that had to remain until they were collected later in the afternoon. He told me that I could go home but I offered to stay to entertain the children who remained. At lunch time I walked down to Haydn Road school about half a mile away and the conditions were treacherous with people saying the buses would stop running.

When I arrived I found that the staff and most of the children had been sent home and the Head Master had gathered the pupils that remained in the large hall. The Headmaster told me that he and I were going to keep these children going until they would be collected at six o'clock. I did not like the way he spoke to me so I replied 'Well perhaps you are but I'm not' and I left. If he had asked me nicely I would have stayed but he didn't and I just got home before the buses stopped running.

In the following years Miss Littlewood wanted me to become a teacher because I'd been a Sunday School teacher from being 15 to when I got married

The School Pianist – Iris Broughton

at 23 and I used to play the piano there every Sunday. I was happy being a school pianist and told her that I did not want to be a teacher. When I left Sunday School at 23 I started to take students and teach piano because I had got my degree. I did get a girl as far as grade 8, she then married an American and her mother-in-law sent all her music over, rolled up like newspapers, because they got it cheaper in America.

So the first school was 'Walter Halls Primary', where I did Monday, Wednesday and Friday all day. And then on Tuesday morning and Thursday morning I went to Seely Junior School on Perry Road in Nottingham. The Head Teacher there was Ken Martin who was a big name in the swimming world. Years later, a large pool was built called 'The Ken Martin Swimming Pool'. (It has now been developed as the Ken Martin Leisure Centre). Ken's wife was a school pianist and when they did music festivals Ken asked me to be the pianist for the combined schools. The festivals were held at the Walter Halls School, and numbers had to be restricted because of the size of the hall. There were 40 people from eight schools, Walter Halls, Seely, Bath Street, a Catholic School (where I also worked) and four more. I used to go along in my lunch break to teach some of the children to play the recorder and I accompanied them on the piano when they played in the festival.

I loved Christmas, I loved the term from October to Christmas, because at all the schools, wherever I went, we were doing carols and every school was doing different ones and it was marvellous. Walter Halls was the one I loved the most because Mary Littlewood did a marvellous play to go with the carols and the children used to learn every carol. They used to know all the words without any papers and this particular one, they did it at night time. I would imagine about half past six when the parents could go in and watch. Dennis and Wallis volunteered to stand at the door and collected threepence from the parents which included admission and a programme. The children then were in a group by the piano, there was a lovely stage there. Miss Littlewood had four children dressed as choirboys, they went outside of the building, came in at the back, carrying a lit candle and walked very slowly down the middle aisle and up onto the stage. As they walked they sang and they had to do it perfectly, step by step. These were the words they said:-

My Dream Job

How far is it to Bethlehem?
Not very far
Shall we find a stable room
Lit by a Star
Can we see the little child
Is he within?
If we lift the wooden latch
May we go in?

When I was fifty-one I was made redundant. All the pianists and nursery nurses were being scrapped as part of a Government plan to save money. Some of the nursery nurses got other jobs easily but I didn't. They offered me a job working in the kitchens but I refused it and did not work for a some time, I can't remember how long. It was probably only a few months but I missed doing the job that I loved.

The Seely Junior School organised two concerts to mark the end of my career and presented me with gifts to mark my enforced retirement. It was reported in the Nottingham Evening Post with a picture on Friday 7th October 1979. This is the report that was included:-

A Nottingham Junior School has held concerts that could be the last of their kind for a while. Because of cuts in education spending, the pianist of the Seely Junior School in Perry Road, Mrs. Iris Broughton, of Somersby Road, Woodthorpe, is being made redundant – so the school organised the special concerts in appreciation of her 18 years service.

Normally the shows take place in July, and the tribute concerts have been rushed through in four weeks.

On the right are Sharon O'Dell and Tom Goldsmith, both aged 10, who presented a silver salver and candelabra to Mrs Broughton on behalf of parents and pupils.

The entertainment consisted of performances from former pupils of the school and a choir and orchestra picked from the last 10 years concerts.

Headmaster Mr. Peter Galloway said it may be the last time such a musical event could be held at the school for a while. "Without a pianist, I don't see how we can keep up the high standard of music we have achieved in previous years" he says.

And as a further indication of the popularity of Mrs Broughton, the shows – held on Wednesday and again last night – were sold out for both nights.

The School Pianist – Iris Broughton

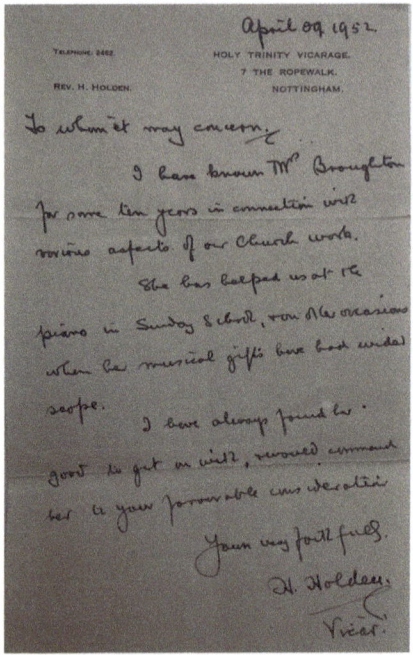
A reference from the Vicar

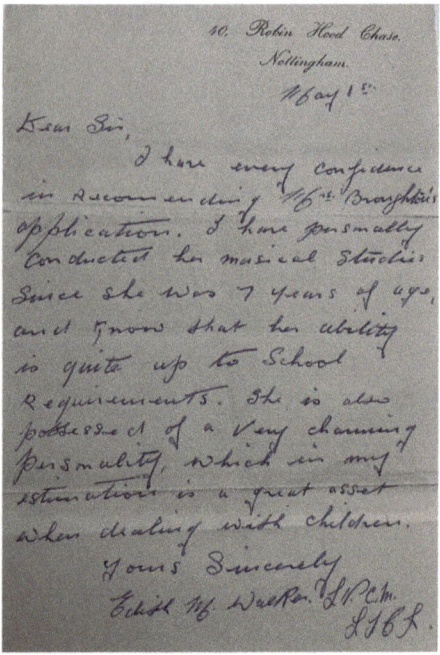
A reference from Iris's Music Teacher

Iris with children she had taught to play Recorders

My Dream Job

Iris at one of the Seely School Concerts

A Nottingham Post heading

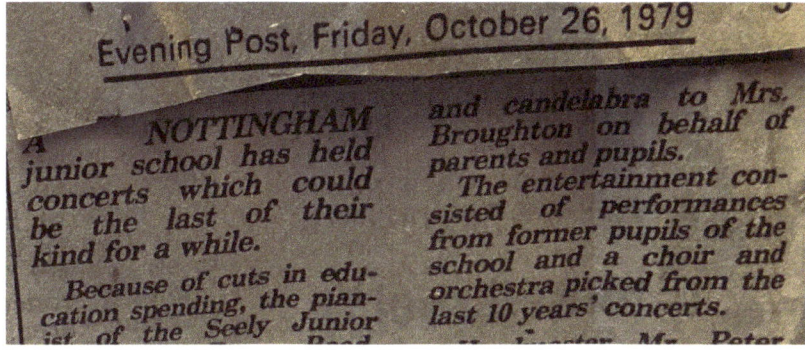

Part of the newspaper story

Some of the sign boards of places where Iris worked, pictured in 2024

Me pictured at Bluebell Infant School

Chapter 4

Resuming my Career

I did not work for some time after being made redundant but, one morning I received a telephone call from a man who used to be Deputy Headmaster at Wolds Hall School, he asked if we could meet at my house to discuss something over a cup of coffee. His name was Alan Smith, after I was made redundant he had moved on to a Headship at Bluebell Primary School. He told me that all the pianists were being reinstated, and asked me if I would go to his school. This was in the November, ready for Christmas and I said 'Yes please, I would love to.' I only knew him on the Staff but I soon got to know all the others. I loved working at Bluebell Primary and resumed working at all the other the schools where I had previously worked. Alan Smith was a good man and continued to come to see me after he retired but when he was 73 he fell down some stairs, banged his head and tragically died from his injuries.

Dennis started work early in the morning so he was usually at home when I got back from work. One afternoon I got home to find him in a terrible state. He tried to tell me what happened but was so upset that it was difficult to understand him. Eventually the story emerged that a lady that he was delivering milk to on the Clifton housing estate, had come out of her house to pay him. She was trying to avoid the dog barking and waking her teenage daughter who was in bed. Turning round to go back into the house she fell over a strap on one of her sandals and the milk bottle that she was carrying broke and caused a terrible bleed to her neck. Dennis shouted for help and for someone with a telephone to call an ambulance. It was futile because the lady had severed the jugular vein and died almost immediately. He had to wake the daughter and tell her that her mother had suffered an accident. As Dennis was talking to me I noticed that one of his eyes was bright red, the shock had caused an acute condition and our son Neil had to come round to put drops in it three times a day for many weeks. Dennis was off work for some time, he could not bend down because of the eye problem. I can't remember how long, but the Co-op continued to pay him while he was off. He had to attend an inquest into the death of the lady and they accepted that Dennis was not responsible but I do know that he had nightmares about it for years afterwards. We were both really sorry for the lady and her family, Dennis had known them for years because he had worked the Clifton area for so long.

A few years later the Nottingham Co-op started negotiations with the milk delivery roundsmen about a scheme involving them becoming self employed and paying a large sum of money to the Co-op for them to buy their rounds. Although Dennis and I had saved some money over the years we didn't like the idea of investing it in the scheme especially as he was about three years from retirement age. He asked about taking early retirement instead and they allowed him to retire a little early in October 1990. The Nottingham Evening Post published two pictures and an article about his final day at work. This is what reporter Paul Coffey wrote about the occasion. He used the heading:-

Street bids farewell to 'our Dennis' By Paul Coffey

Popular milkman Dennis Broughton was given an emotional farewell on his final round by residents of a Clifton street. He was retiring after 28 years of delivering 'pintas' in the area and people on Bournmoor Avenue came out in numbers to say "Thank you".

A collection was organised by Mrs Sylvia Bear and Mrs Hazel Marshall to buy Dennis a present.

Mrs Bear said: "Dennis is a wonderful man and he has been a friend to a lot of people for a long time. For many residents on the street, including myself, he has been the only milkman we have ever had. We are all going to miss him. It is a mark of his popularity that we collected enough money to buy him a camera and a bouquet of flowers for his wife Iris."

Mrs Lily Fisher said: "Everyone will miss him because he always had time for a joke and smile. Whenever you were feeling down he was a real tonic."

Mrs Dorothy Goffin joined in the praise. She said "There will never be another like Dennis. He was a friend to us all."

The man himself seemed a little overwhelmed with the flattery but still found time to joke with some of the residents.

"I'm amazed that they have gone to all the trouble for me. It's a really nice gesture. It has been great working this round for the past 28 years because I have had the best set of customers one could hope for. Although I will miss the job it will be nice to put my feet up by doing some fishing." Mr Broughton lives on Somersby Road, Woodthorpe with his wife Iris.

Resuming my Career

I continued working for two more years after Dennis retired and then it was time for me to retire. The Headmaster, Frank Knowles and School Secretary Joan Whitehall combined to organise a retirement party at Walter Halls Primary School on Thursday 16 July 1992. They invited lots of people and these are some of the letters we received. (I have left the addresses out for privacy reasons).

Nottingham 13-7-92

Dear Frank

Thank you for the invitation to the retirement party you are organising for Iris on Thursday.

I shall be very happy to come.

It really is full circle. I first met Iris when I joined the Staff at Walter Halls in 1963 and for the next 22 years, at your school and later at Seely, had the great pleasure of working with her. She was never just a 'visiting pianist' but always thought of as a member of Staff. This gave me the opportunity to appreciate through our long association, just how great a contribution she has made to the musical life of schools in our part of the City.

To the individual schools in which she worked Iris gave unstinting support, in, and out of school hours. Her modest suggestions, tactful advice and help to teachers of singing enabled us to develop a love of music in our pupils. A very important part of that was in bringing to ones attention to what was being done in other schools. Many of the songs which became my firm favourites (and the children I taught) came through Iris, from other schools whose teachers were far more musical than I.

One also remembers the various Music Festivals — area schools, local and City — in which she played for us. It must have meant many hours of practice preparing the selected pieces to the high standard of accompaniment (which drew appreciative comments from adjudicators). Moral support to a nervous conductor on those occasions was enormous-I remember telling my choir-"If I go wrong in conducting, just follow Mrs Broughton and I'll catch up with you!

Altogether, Iris has been a big influence in our schools' musical lives and I trust that this will be recognised on Thursday.

Finally, may I, through you, wish her every happiness in her retirement.

Yours sincerely, Peter Galloway

The School Pianist – Iris Broughton

From Mary H Littlewood (Former Headmistress of Walter Halls School)
Stapleford, Nottingham 30 June 1992

Dear Mr Knowles

Thank you for your invitation to Iris's Retirement Party. I shall be pleased to accept.

Iris came to me at the Walter Halls in the very first week of her career as a school pianist, and we have kept in touch ever since. I am glad to know that you, to, value her-as a pianist and as a person.

I hope you won't mind if I bring my cousin with me. He constantly ferries me about, and he will be glad to join in tributes to her. I enclose a cheque from both of us.

Yours sincerely, Mary H Littlewood

From Mrs Syson
5 July 1992

Dear Frank

I am very pleased to accept your kind invitation to Iris's retirement party on Thursday 16 July in the school hall at 4.00pm.

I am looking forward, very much, to seeing you all once again and once again being "in School." Please find enclosed cheque as a contribution towards a gift for Iris.

Yours sincerely, Brenda

From Mrs Suggitt
East Bridgford
July 1992

Dear Mr Knowles

Thank you for the invitation to Iris's retirement party. I shall be delighted to attend.

I enclose a cheque for her present.

Yours sincerely, Ivy Suggitt

Resuming my Career

Mapperley
Nottingham 6 July 1992

Thank you for the invitation to Iris's retirement party. I look forward to seeing her again and enclose a cheque to contribute to a present.

Marion Church

Wollaton
Nottingham
July 1992

Dear Mr Knowles

I shall be delighted to attend Iris's retirement party for with her help and advice I not only improved my music abilities but gained a friend. Please accept my contribution towards a gift and I look forward to seeing you all on Thursday 16 July.

Yours sincerely Edna Hogg

Sherwood
Nottingham 13 July 1992

Dear Frank

I was delighted to receive your note inviting me to Iris's retirement party. Unfortunately I'm unable to attend owing to a prior commitment.

However, I'm delighted to be able to contribute to a present-please find cheque enclosed. I can't think of many other school pianists who have worked so hard for the children and staff of her respective schools over so many years.

Please pass on my very best wishes to Iris and Dennis for a long and happy retirement.

I know that in my professional career I owe Iris a debt of gratitude for all the help she's given — particularly to those of us, like me, who have no special musical leanings.

Yours sincerely Peter Littlewood

St Annes
Nottingham

Dear Mr Knowles

Thank you for your letter, I would very much like to come to Iris's retirement party.

The School Pianist – Iris Broughton

Iris is a lovely lady, I have been Blue Belle Hills lollipop lady for over 20 years and not once did she not come to me fo a chat. – no matter what the weather.

Also thank you very much for doing this kind thing for her. I enclose £5 for your school funds. Look forward to meeting you.

Yours sincerely Shiela Sims

Carlton
Nottingham

Dear Mr Knowles

Thank you for the invitation to Iris Broughton's retiring party. I have known Iris for many years, and look forward to seeing her on 16 July. I enclose my donation.

Yours sincerely, Ada Drury

Radcliffe-on-Trent
Nottingham

Dear Frank

Thank you very much for your letter about Iris's retirement party. I would love to come and enclose a contribution towards her present. Looking forward to seeing you then.

Love, Sue (Conway)

Wollaton
Nottingham

Dear Iris

I have just heard from Frank about your retirement. Thank you for the invitation to your party! I wouldn't miss it for anything.

I shall always be grateful to you for your help and encouragement throughout all my years at Walter Halls. The thought of doing a concert without your help would have been daunting. Throughout the years you have become a mine of information and I for one have been very glad of your suggestions and experience.

The school, and the other schools you went to, will miss you greatly too.

I hope you and Dennis will enjoy many years of retirement together.

With Love, Doreen (Stean)

Resuming my Career

Here are the words of a song they sang at the party, they used the tune of 'My Darling Clementine'.

Mrs Broughton, Mrs Broughton
You are leaving us today
What will we do, for our concerts
When we've not got you to play?

On a Tuesday and a Thursday
When the children want to sing
Without you to play piano
Staff can't play a blooming thing!

Mrs Broughton, Mrs Broughton
The whole choir will miss you too
Mrs Murphy does her best now
But she's not as good as you

Mrs Broughton, you've spare time now
You could always go to Venice
Or stay at home and weed the garden
Making cups of tea for Dennis

Mrs Broughton, Mrs Broughton
We will miss you very much
One last favour, as you go now
Just make sure you keep in touch.

It was a great party and School Secretary, Joan Whitehall, collected photographs and letters which she put in my 'Retirement Photograph Album' and presented it to me later.

The School Pianist – Iris Broughton

Dennis on his last Milk Round before retiring

Street bids farewell to 'our Dennis'

By PAUL COFFEY

POPULAR milkman Dennis Broughton was given an emotional farewell on his final round by residents of a Clifton street. He was retiring after 28 years of delivering pintas in the area and people on Bournmoor Avenue came out in numbers to say "thank you".

A collection was organised by Mrs Sylvia Bear and Mrs Hazel Marshall to buy Dennis a present.

Mrs Bear said: "Dennis is a wonderful man and he has been a friend to a lot of people for a long time.

"For many residents on the street, including myself, he has been the only milkman we have ever had. We are all going to miss him.

The man himself seemed a little overwhelmed with the flattery but still found time to joke with some of the residents.

"I'm amazed that they have gone to all

A cutting from the Nottingham Evening Post

With some of his customers

Where Iris started the second phase of her career

The album calligraphy

The School Pianist – Iris Broughton

Iris and Dennis

Iris with piano appeared as a cake decoration

Chapter 5

Retirement

After Dennis retired he had joined the British Legion and went once a month on a Monday night to the one in Arnold. They used to have annual Remembrance Day services at St Pauls Church on Mansfield Road Daybrook and Dennis had to get up in the pulpit and speak. He was very nervous about that because he had never spoken in public before. I attended those services and was very proud of Dennis because I knew how worried he was about the task. I joined the Ladies section when I retired and used to go once a month on a Tuesday.

Dennis started going to classes for painting at St Judes Church Hall, Mapperley and brought some of his work home which is displayed around the house. He got involved with setting up the tables and helped to organise the painting group so he became very busy.

After the activity of my retirement party and finishing work I soon felt a bit bored and lacked inspiration. Someone I knew suggested that I should join a singing group that she was in, the problem was that it was about four miles away. My friend said there was a spare seat in the car that she went in and she would ask if they would take me, the answer was, Yes, so I joined the Netherfield Singers as a Choir member. It was a mixed choir and Geoff, the pianist was experiencing loss of hearing and wanted to give up. He knew me and immediately asked if I would adopt his role and I agreed. We did rehearsals once a week and various concerts and I really enjoyed being back playing the piano again and doing the concerts.

In May 1995, nearly three years after I retired, a terrible tragedy happened which brought back memories of Walter Halls Primary School flooding back to me. The School Secretary was Joan Whitehall who was an experienced narrow boat user and had organised school trips on the boats. On this occasion twenty children, ten girls, ten boys, and three teachers were on a three week adventure using two hired barges. They had set out from Braunstone in Leicestershire on 6 May 1995 and were planning to finish the second leg of the three part trip in Northampton. At 8-30am on Sunday 14 May 1995 some of the children were eating breakfast inside the leading barge and others were on the other barge, following close behind. Mrs Whitehall was wearing a sheepskin jacket and was standing at the stern and steering the boat round a sharp, tight, bend on the canal. She had put the engine into reverse and apparently slipped and fell into the water. She was sucked into the propellor and trapped. Two teachers from the second boat, from the same school, tried to rescue her, they were helped by two workmen, from the nearby M6 roadworks, but it was in vain. Her body was recovered later by the Fire Brigade, using breathing apparatus. All the children were taken to Queens Road Police Station in Birmingham and looked after until a coach arrived to take them back to Nottingham. An eye witness said, 'I think she was at the back of the boat and was trying to reverse it back a bit when she must have slipped. It looked like she was being pulled under. She was struggling and screaming. Some of the children were looking through the windows down the aisle of the barge when she fell overboard and they were crying'.

Yesterday police officers were on board the boats, collecting bags containing the pupils belongings. A West Midlands police officer said 'It was a lovely school trip and it is tragic that something so horrific could happen'. Two other canal trippers told how they travelled behind the school party for three days before the tragedy. One of them said 'They all seemed pretty well behaved and were having a wonderful time, laughing with each other'. A Nottinghamshire County Council spokesman said 'Mrs Whitehall had been Secretary at the 380 pupil Walter Halls Primary School in Querneby Road, Mapperley, Nottingham for 10 years. Staff and pupils are still shocked. They are still trying to come to terms with this tragic loss to the school'. Joan Whitehall was a much loved and respected member of Staff. (I am indebted to The Herald Newspaper 15th May 1995 and the Nottingham Evening Post of the same date for information used in this story and for permission to use the picture MP).

A few weeks later a Memorial Service was held at St Judes Church, Woodborough Road Mapperley and I was honoured to play piano during the service. I had known Joan Whitehall for many years and she had helped to organise my retirement party. She had done the lovely calligraphy in my photograph album. It was the tragic end of the School Secretary who we all loved.

In Autumn 2000 Dennis and I received an invitation to attend a Rededication Ceremony of the Ship, HMS Nottingham, a Destroyer that had just been refitted at a cost of £42 million. We were honoured to be invited because of our work for the British Legion and were among a group of Nottingham residents who were invited. The ceremony was arranged for Friday 9 February 2001 so

Retirement

there was plenty of time to organise what we would wear. The day before the ceremony we boarded a luxury coach in Nottingham and were taken to a hotel in Portsmouth overnight because the event started early the next day. We boarded the coach after breakfast the next morning and were taken to a reception in a huge marquee at the Victory Jetty Naval Base, close to HMS Victory. It was well organised with everyone allocated reserved tables. The man who sat next to me was the father of the Captain and he was very interesting to talk to. We were then escorted to seats to enjoy the Royal Marine Band and parade followed by the Rededication Ceremony. We were then escorted aboard HMS Nottingham and shown certain parts of the ship. It was a really interesting experience which we both enjoyed. It was finished by mid afternoon and we boarded our coach for the long journey back to Nottingham.

About eighteen months later, on 7 July 2002, we learned that HMS Nottingham had been badly damaged after hitting a large rock east of Australia. Newspaper reports stated that a 160 foot hole was torn down the side of the ship from bow to bridge flooding five of the compartments and nearly causing the ship to sink. The damage was severe and the ship was not brought back to British waters until December of that year. Dennis followed the story and told me the Captain and some officers of the ship were Court Martialled and severely disciplined. (The details of the Court Martial are available on the World Wide Web MP). I remembered talking to the father of Commander Richard Farrington and felt very sorry for what had happened because of my personal meeting with his father. HMS Nottingham was eventually decommissioned and sold for scrap in 2011.

As time progressed all the male members of the Netherfield Singers died or left the choir so only a few ladies remained. Tom Butcher, the husband of the lady who took me to Netherfield founded a ladies choir which was called the Rose Singers so we joined that group and got many concert engagements.

Dennis became very ill and died on 15 June 2009. He was 81 years of age, we had been married for over 58 years. I was lost without him but the family did their best to support me by looking after me and taking me on holidays at Christmas time. Dennis had a computer and for many years he had done copies of music or songs and made programmes for me. I had never learned to use the computer so could not do it myself. I didn't realise how much I missed him for that. He used to drive me to the shops, Choir rehearsals and concerts. He had always been there for me and I was lost without him. The Choir became an even bigger part of my life. I invited my cousin Joan and her husband Michael to one of

The School Pianist – Iris Broughton

our concerts and he told me that he could make a video of our next performance and load it to something that he called YouTube. I did not know anything about that so spoke to Tom Butcher and Choir members about it, they were in favour so I asked Michael to video at our next concert. Some ladies in the Choir told me that they had seen themselves on YouTube but I never fathomed out how to watch them. I was suffering hearing loss and gradually stopped playing the piano but was asked to conduct the Choir in a few concerts. It was frustrating at times because sometimes the pianist did not perform to my liking but I could not play piano and conduct at same time.

One of the funniest things we did with the Rose Singers was a comedy song called 'Looking for a Man'. We performed it at the Netherfield and Colwick Senior Citizens Club in the Bethesda Church, Community Hall in Netherfield. We had rehearsed there for many years. Michael has put it on YouTube and I have given him permission to write his own chapter to explain about that.

During the last five months Michael and I have been working on this book and hope that you are enjoying reading it.

Iris walking in the British Legion parade

Retirement

Joan had been School Secretary for ten years

Me and Dennis in Malta, who could forget those buses?

The School Pianist – Iris Broughton

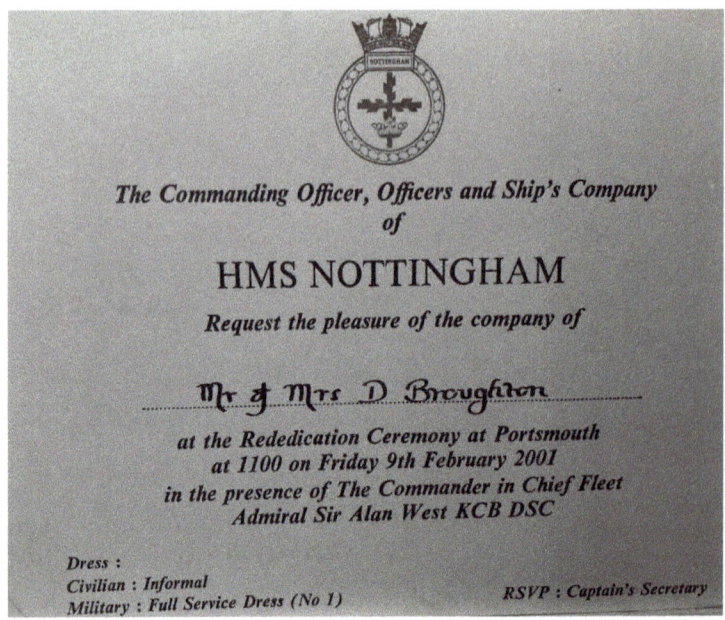

The invitation

Iris enjoyed talking to the Father of Commander Farrington

Early Years

The Netherfield Singers

Me with Danielle Hall at a Rose singers concert

Chapter 6

by Neil Broughton

My Mother and Father, Iris and Dennis

My name is Neil Broughton, I was born on 7 July 1955 and enjoyed a very happy childhood with my Mother, Iris and Father Dennis. We lived in a terraced house on Wellington Street which is just off Huntingdon Street, very close to the centre of Nottingham and near to the Victoria Railway Station. There were two stations in Nottingham at that time but the one near us was closed in September 1967 leaving the Midland Station as the only mainline station in the City. We lived next door to Mothers brother, Wallis and his wife Dorothy. Of course I knew them as Uncle Wallis and Auntie Dorothy and they had two sons, Paul who was two years older than me and Ian who was six months older. Me and my cousins were inseparable, I can remember that there was a wall in the back garden between the two houses and the wall was knocked down so that we could walk out of our back door and into next door so we lads could be together.

My earliest childhood memory is sitting in a pram facing backwards, towards my mother whilst my cousin Ian was facing forwards in his being pushed by Auntie Dorothy. I wanted to be facing forward like Ian. We were often wheeled in our prams to the shops at Hockley which is about half a mile from where we lived. I was Christened as a youngster and my Mother was very proud that the Vicar put a picture of me in the vicarage. When I was four or five I can remember a birthday party when I was running round the kitchen and fell and banged my head on the corner of the hearth so had to have stitches just above my eye. We went on holiday just afterwards and with me having a bandage on my head and a big dressing over my eye.

My father was a welder and one occasion he broke a bone in his foot at work and had to go to hospital. I can remember my parents being annoyed because he was taken 'off the clock' the minute he left work and did not get any money until he went back again. Because of this Dad became a shop steward and tried to get better conditions for the workers. This led to strained relationship between him and the management so he decided to work for the Co-op as a milkman like Uncle Wallis. This was good for me because he started work early in the morning and often took me fishing with him when I finished school in the afternoon. On one occasion it was extremely cold and I helped Dad to break the ice on the river before he started fishing. My hands were very cold but I enjoyed the time spent with my father, he told stories about his National Service. In those days young men were conscripted into one of the armed services for two years at eighteen years of age. Dad was in the Army and served in India, he told me about one occasion when a lot of men were forced to do a very long walk in extremely hot and hilly conditions and he was one of only four who finished. Some of the soldiers had blood running out of the lace holes of their boots but were forced to keep going. He played football for the regiment in India so was obviously a fit young man. When I was young I can remember Dad decorating a downstairs room one Saturday afternoon. He was finishing in the late afternoon and asked Mum to put the television on so he could listen to the football results. As she touched the electrical socket there was a loud bang and she got a shock, probably because the wall was wet from the painting. One of her hands was badly burned and she had to go to hospital for regular treatment. That was when she was working as a hairdresser so she had to have time off work but the medical people managed to get her hand better without permanent damage.

Later on Mother got a full time job as a school pianist and at that time they had very long lunch breaks so I used to go to my grandma's house every day, she made lovely food and I didn't want school dinners. Mother used to give private lessons in the evenings and I had to be quiet while this was going on. She tried to teach me to play piano but I was more interested in being out with my friends so would not stick at it though I loved hearing her play. There were about fifty children in my class and perhaps I did not work as hard as I should have done at school though I loved playing football. They used to make us walk to 'The Forest' the local recreation ground, one time home of Nottingham Forest FC. We walked in crocodile formation but there was no organisation when we got there so we just kicked balls about as we pleased. Father was not very impressed with this because he was a good amateur footballer and played for Basford United, he was often mentioned in the Nottingham Football Post for his goal scoring exploits. He had a trial with a football league club but nothing came of it.

In the 1960s I liked the Beatles and wanted a guitar for Christmas so I could be like them. To my disappointment I got a Banjo instead, Mum was not pleased when I said, 'I wanted to be like John Lennon, not George Formby'.

The School Pianist – Iris Broughton

On leaving school my first job title was Optical Mechanic at Gray & Bull, Opticians of Pelham Street, in Nottingham. I was fitting lenses into spectacle frames but as a new employee I had to do other things as well. One of my responsibilities was to look after a coke boiler in the winter but one day I left the chimney damper in and forgot about it until someone came round from the fur shop next door and said that smoke was coming into their premises. I immediately pulled the damper out but someone had called the fire brigade so I was in trouble and called into Mr Bull's office. He stuttered and I can remember him stammering 'You are a B-B-B blithering idiot B-B-B Broughton'. I did not get the sack but decided to look for another job and became a watchmaker at Nottingham Horological Services, this was run by a man who took repairs in from various local businesses. I did a correspondence course in addition to the training I received and became quite good at it. After about four years he retired and I got a job doing watch repairs at Allen Jewellers which I enjoyed. Whilst I was there the husband of one of the ladies who worked there was selling a car which I bought for fifty pounds. It was one of the original Mini's with external door hinges and solenoid starter on the floor. My cousin Paul taught me how to drive it up and down the drive outside my parents house. He was very interested in cars and went on to work as an Auto Electrician. I did not hit the wall so was pleased with myself and booked six driving lessons. They were unusual because the instructor bought fish and chips before he picked me up and sat eating them, as I was doing my lessons. I passed my test first time so started to go out in the car with my cousins, Ian and Paul.

Some of my friends worked as telephone engineers and I decided I wanted to do that because of the outdoor life compared with being inside all the time. I applied and found it was part of the General Post Office Group, they had no vacancies, but gave me work as a postman driver, working on a three shift system. I did that for some time until a vacancy became available on the telecom side. The interview and tests were stringent but I passed and achieved my ambition to be a BT engineer. I really enjoyed that job especially when, on two occasions, I was sent to the BT Training Centre at Bletchley Park. This is part of a huge Exhibition area in Milton Keynes, built around Britain's World War Two Codebreakers, GCHQ (Government Communications Head Quarters). BT is the Sole and Exclusive Corporate Partner of the restoration of the Teleprinter Building and Exhibition. I felt proud to be working for British Telecom which I did for 28 years until my retirement.

Since I retired we try to get away on holidays or short breaks or even days out. I have been researching the Family tree and have a couple of motorbikes. I have done Mums garden for around the last 15 or so years and have been helping to care for her over the last ten years. This has become progressively more time consuming and difficult as she has got older.

When she said she wanted to write a book it did not unduly surprise me as she has always had the personality to try new things and be actively doing things. I feel honoured to have been asked to provide a contribution to her book.

Dad, the amateur footballer

Neil posing while painting at parents house

The job has brought him to his knees

Neil's first set of wheels

My Aunty Iris

Chapter 7

by Paul Parker

My Aunty Iris

My name is Paul Parker, I am one of two sons of Wallis and Dorothy Parker, I was born in 1953 and my younger brother, Ian in 1955. My parents were very close to Aunty Iris and Uncle Dennis so I have known Iris, who is the sister of my father Wallis, for as long as I can remember. Christmas was a special time for her and she loved the school Carol concerts. Christmas and Easter were always spent with the immediate family, at one house one day and the other house the next. Neil was the son of Iris and Dennis and he was born in 1955 so we lads were of similar age. As we grew up, on Boxing Day we all met at a local pub and then went back to our family house on Barden Road for lunch. The fun would start with Dennis getting dressed up or playing a trick on someone. The jokes continued with a new game every year and card games.

We also had summer holidays together in Cornwall, Wales and the Lake District, where we all got a shock staying in a shack on a farm miles down a dirt track and the toilet in the farm yard. A torch was supplied. The only saving grace was that it was that hot summer of 1975. Many happy evenings were spent together, playing darts etcetera, with a party 7 plus fish and chips. In September 1978 Iris was devastated by the sudden death of her brother, Wallace (my Father) of a heart attack at 56 years old.

Iris and Dennis both liked Scotland and had many holidays touring in their car. They also had holidays at her friends flat on the beach front at Los Boliches, near Fuengirola, Spain. Neil and Jaki joined them on many occasions, Neil would hire a car so they could see more of the Costa Del Sol. Iris and my mother Dorothy were good friends and would see each other for coffee most days. Iris missed her chats with Dorothy when she died after the family had spent Boxing Day together in 2001.

The year 2009 was a sad one for our whole family when Dennis died of cancer followed by close relatives, Ann, Larry and my brother, Ian, suddenly of a heart attack, at 54 years old. After this Iris, Neil, Jaki and I could not face Christmas at home and decided to go away to Fuengirola, Spain. This started a theme which continued until 2019. The following year, 2010, the four of us returned to Fuengirola for Christmas and the New Year. Iris and I continued to go abroad for Christmas, visiting Tunisia twice, Lanzarote twice, Gran Canaria, Fuerteventura and Egypt. Iris enjoyed the warm and sunny weather and her favourite hobby of talking and making new friends. She liked the all inclusive hotels where she would get the waiters running around after her. On one trip to Hammamet, Tunisia, a gentleman took a fancy to her and wrote to her for a while. Iris has a sense of fun and would tell people that me, Paul, was her Toy Boy. The hotel Fuerteventura was in the South part of the island which was full of Germans. Iris did not like it as she had no one to talk to so she talked me into going for an evening out, a meal and show. It turned out to be a drag show and when they got me up on stage, she could not stop laughing. It made her holiday. Iris was shocked when Santa arrived on the beach of Sharm, Egypt, on a camel and knocked on the door of her room on Christmas Eve, with a stocking full of sweets etcetera.

With Neil and me still working, 4 day breaks with Shearings on Easter and Bank holidays was popular with Iris, Neil, Jaki and me, as nobody had to drive. Long coach drives to Cornwall and the Isle of Wight were tiring but the South coast, Scarborough and Cotswolds all made good breaks away. Iris loved her holidays on three cruises, two in the Mediterranean and one in the Baltic for Neils 60th Birthday in 2015. She soon made herself at home, going to talks and concerts on board ship. Her favourite part was getting dressed up for the formal evenings.

Iris wanted to go away one more time so at Christmas 2021, She and I went to the Spa Town of Buxton in Derbyshire. Iris had a walk round Bakewell and viewed the snow in Buxton on Boxing Day. By 2022, at 94 years of age, going on holidays was getting a bit too much for Iris so that was the last time we went away together.

My brother Ian who did not live to enjoy retirement holidays

Iris with me and entertainers

Chapter 8

by Joan Parkinson

My Cousin – Iris Broughton

My name is Joan Parkinson, these are memories of my cousin, Iris Broughton, who was a school pianist but played the piano on family visits. My favourite was 'Rudolph the Red Nosed Reindeer' and I used to drive her mad by asking her to play it over and over again. I remember Iris's mother, Aunty Kitty (Catherine) cutting the hair of my sister Ann and me. She also made most of our clothes as she was a very good dressmaker. My sister, Ann and I were bridesmaids for Iris and Dennis when I was 3 years old. I can remember Iris's father, Uncle Herbert, taking us home in his van and singing 'Roses of Picardy' as he was driving along.

At fifteen yers of age I started work in the textile trade at Broad Marsh in Nottingham but the business moved to Clifton when the building was demolished to make way for a bus station. I then went to the Art College in Nottingham on day release for one day each week. The College was situated on Waverley Street at that time and the two sessions were from 10am to 4pm and 7pm to 9 pm. It was too far to go home to Broxtowe so I used go to my family Iris, Dorothy, and Iris's Mother, Catherine for tea and relaxation. They all lived a short walk from the College on Wellington Street and Shelton Street. After tea we listened to records on an old radiogram with my cousins, Paul, Ian and Neal before I went back to College. I remember one evening we went round to Iris's mothers house on Shelton Street and had to sit very quiet because Iris was giving a piano lesson to a pupil.

I can remember my family staying in a caravan for a week at Cleethorpes, on the Lincolnshire coast, Iris and her family visited us for one day. Over the years there have been family reunions. I got married to Michael Parkinson, we went to live at Keyworth and developed an interest in sequence dancing. Many years later we started taking his parents out for a drive on Saturday evenings. Michael was interested that Iris had a piano at home and had loads of music so asked her if we could go there one evening for her to play the piano to us. We discovered what a special lady Iris is because when we arrived she had put on a huge selection of food for us to enjoy for supper later on. The food was in the lounge but first Iris took us into an adjoining room where an upright piano was situated. There was music on tables, piled on the floor in big heaps, on top of the piano and on shelves. There was all sorts of music, sheets, books and hand written papers situated all around the room. Iris invited us to find what we wanted her to play and it was magic. The doors between the two rooms were slid open and Iris proceeded to play what we had selected. Of course it had to start with Rudolph. We were delighted to find a sheet of music called 'The Maxina', one of our favourite dances. As the evening developed I realised that Dennis was showing signs of tiredness. He was a milk delivery roundsman and had to get up at 4 o clock the following morning even though it was Sunday. We stopped to have supper but it was still nearly 11 pm when we left so I felt very guilty about Dennis, a lovely man who we all liked. Iris was working as a school pianist so did not have to go to work the following day. We continued to enjoy those musical evenings at intervals of about six months and marvelled that Iris played whatever we found even though she had not played some of them for many years.

The years slipped by and Dennis retired followed by Iris a couple of years later. She became the Musical Director of a choir called the Rose Singers and invited us to go to a St George's Day concert at Carlton. Michael had booked a train ticket to London for that day so my nephew Steven took me and brought me home. It turned out to be a very posh event organised by the Nottinghamshire branch of the Royal Society of St George, the venue was the Richard Herod Centre, Carlton, Nottingham on Wednesday 23 April 2014. When we arrived I heard the familiar voice of Colin Slater who was the commentator on the Notts County matches for Radio Nottingham, we learned that he was appointed the new President of the Nottinghamshire Royal Society of St George that very evening. Colin spoke to Steven and me in a very friendly manner and was impressed that we were family members of Iris Broughton who he knew as the Musical Director of the Rose Singers. They had been booked by the group to perform a concert that evening which Iris introduced as well as directed and we felt very proud of her. This was what they included in their programme:-

The School Pianist – Iris Broughton

St George's Day Concert
Part One

The Rose Singers of Carlton U3A
Musical Director – Iris Broughton
Accompanist – Geoff Smith
It's a Grand Night for Singing
Tonight
Can You Feel the Love Tonight?
Solo – Barbara Buxton
Any Dream Will Do
I Dreamed a Dream
I Enjoy Being a Girl, Got no Diamond,
Diamonds are a Girls Best Friend
Poem – Sheila Fisher
'I'm all right'
Oom – Pah Pah and Who Will Buy My Sweet Red Roses (From Oliver)
The Rose (Choir Signature Song)

There was then a break before the choir performed Part Two

Choir with Audience Participation
Keep the Home Fires Burning
Pack Up your Troubles
It's a Long Way To Tipperary
Hallo! Hallo! Who's Your Lady Friend
Roses of Picardy
Jerusalem
I Vow To Thee My Country
There'll Always Be An England
Rose of England
Song of Liberty
Land of Hope and Glory

It was a fabulous evening and everyone really enjoyed it. We did not know then but it was the first of many concerts that Iris invited us to.

My Cousin – Iris Broughton

Bridesmaids for the wedding of Iris & Dennis, Ann on left, Joan on Right

The Coat of Arms

Chapter 9

My Music Collection

When I retired I had to get rid of most of the books and sheets of music that I had acquired over the years but there were some too treasured to lose. Some had been passed down to me by my Father and just looking at the titles and words brings back so many memories. In this chapter I am listing the titles of the music that mean so much to me starting with sheet music with my nee name, Iris Parker written on the cover.

1 Without a Song – Rose, Eliscue & Youmans, with hand written sheet of words

2 Sleepy Lagoon Words Jack Lawrence Music Eric Coates Chappell & Co Bond St

3 Songs of the Western Isles Song to the Seals & The Bird of St Bride – JB Cramer Bond St

4 Samson and Delilah C. Saint-Saens Paris A.Durand & Co 4 Place de Madeleine 2 copies

5 Spring in my Heart – Words Ralph Freed Music Johann Strauss – Deanna Durbin – Film

6 They Didn't Believe Me – Words M. E. Rourke Music Jerome D Kern 1914 Harms USA

7 Songs from Stage and Screen – Heaven, I'm in Heaven. Hello Dolly. Any Dream will Do

8 Smile – Words John Turner & Geoffrey Parsons Music Charles Chaplin – Bourne Music

9 Sympathy – Music Rudolf Friml Lyrics Otto Harbach & Gus Kahn, Jeanette MacDonald

10 So Deep is the Night (Tristesse) Words Jean Marietti & Andre Viud Music FR Chopin

My Music Collection

11 Somewhere – Music Leonard Bernstein Lyrics Stephen Sondheim – Boosey & Harkes

12 South of the Border by Jimmy Kennedy and Michael Carr – Peter Morris Music Ltd

13 Sing a Song of Sixpence – A new setting of an old rhyme by J Michael Diack (Handel)

14 Sing a Song of Sixpence – (A second copy)

15 KUMBAYA – Traditional tune harmonised by compilers of New Church Praise (1975)

16 Some Day my Heart will Awake – Lyrics Christopher Hassall Music Ivor Novello

17 Shine Through my Dreams – Words Christopher Hassall Music Ivor Novello, Chappell

18 Santa Lucia – New English Version by Bernard Sydney & Edward McKay, Gracie Fields

19 Sing, Joyous Bird – Words Nora C. Usher Music Montague F. Phillips. Chappell & Co

20 Sanctuary of the Heart Words & Music by Albert W. Ketelbey, Bosworth & Co London

21 Roses of Picardy – Words by Fred Weatherly Music Haydn Wood, Chappell & Co Ltd

From here the music is signed Iris Broughton so it was bought after my marriage in 1951.

22 Santa Lucia, Folk song of Naples, Florence Hoare – Arr Percy Fletcher (Stuck to card)

23 Franz Schubert Songs, The Trout, Die Forelle, Op 32. English version by Richard Capell

24 Stranger in Paradise – Words & Music Robert Wright/George Forrest, Alexander Borodin

25 Schubert's Serenade – Words Charles Wilmote, well used and stuck onto brown card

26 Schubert's Serenade – different publication The B F Wood Music Oxford St London

27 She shall have Music – Words Herbert J. Brandon Music Alan Murray, Chappell & Co

28 Spring Song – Edvard Greig, English words by R.H. Elkin, Edwin Ashdown Ltd, London

29 Somewhere along the Way – Words Sammy Gallop Music Kurt Adams, (Nat King Cole)

30 Send in the Clowns – Stephen Sondheim (A Little Night Music) Rilting Music Inc

31 Rainbow Connection – Paul Williams/Kenny Asher, Why so many songs about Rainbows?

32 Sing a Rainbow – Words and Music by Arthur Hamilton, Red and Yellow and Pink/Green

33 Shalom Chaverim – a Hebrew Folk Song, the music has been stuck on cardboard

34 Amigos Para Siempre, Friends for Life, Theme of the Barcelona 1992 Olympic games

35 The Foggy Foggy Dew. From Suffolk – Handwritten, then printed copy made by Iris

36 In a Monastery Garden – Albert Ketelbey, Characteristic Intermezzo, piano, J.H. Larway

37 Ee By Gum But Am Cowd. – Words/Music John Meeks Colin Radcliffe, Edmund Crotty

38 Somewhere out there – Words & Music James Horner Barry Mann & Cynthia Weil

39 Roses of Picardy (Lower Key) Fred E. Weatherley & Haydn Wood

40 Softly, As I leave You – Words G. Galabreese. English words Hal Shaper Music, Vita

41 My Old Man (Said follow the van) – Words & Music Fred W Leigh and Charles Collins

42 Teddy Bears Picnic – Arrangement copyright 2018 by Alec D Jackson, MD Rose Singers

43 Speed your Journey from the Opera Nabucco – Giuseppe Verdi

Early Years

44 I'd like to Teach the World to Sing – Roger Cook, Handwritten on music lined paper

45 Salad Days – Lyrics Julian Slade & Dorothy Reynolds, Music Julian Slade, Nequests

46 Desert Song – Words Otto Harbach & Oscar Hammerstein II Music Sigmund Romberg

47 Hans Christian Anderson, Children's Album – Words & Music Frank Loesser Nequest's

48 Fiddler on the Roof – Words Sheldon Harnick Music Jerry Bock Book Joseph Stein

49 No Other Love – Words Oscar Hammerstein II Music Richard Rogers, Williamson Music

50 Happy Talk from South Pacific – Words Oscar Hammerstein Music Richard Rogers

51 South Pacific Piano Selection, with lots of hand written text. Williamson Music Ltd

52 My Fair Lady – Words Alan Jay Lerner Music Frederick Lowe, Chappell & Co Ltd

53 Carousel – Words Hammerstein Music Richard Rogers, 5 songs, Williamson Music Ltd

54 Carousel – Words Hammerstein Music Richard Rogers, 8 songs, Williamson Music Ltd

55 Carousel – Words Hammerstein Music Richard Rogers, 5 songs, (album)

56 The King and I – Piano selection, with songs & hand written revisions – music & words

57 The King and I – Song Album (5 songs), Williamson Music – London & New York

58 Oklahoma! Iris Parker with hand written revisions, Williamson & Chappell

59 Oklahoma! Iris Parker with a lot of additional sheet music, Williamson & Chappell

60 Oklahoma! Iris Broughton, Piano Selection (later version than the previous two)

61 Oliver, – Full Score, book, Music & Lyrics by Lionel Bart, Lakeview Music Publishing

62 Oliver – Piano selection, additional sheet music inserted, Columbia pictures, Nequest's

63 Abba – Fifteen easy play piano arrangements including Words. Music Sales Ltd, London

64 Kismet, Selections from, by Robert Wright & George Forest, themes by A. Borodin

65 Kismet, And this is my Beloved – Words & Music Robert Wright & George Forest

66 Kiss Me Kate – Music/words Cole Porter, Book Sam & Bella Spewack, Chappell London

67 Gigi – Piano selection, Words Alan Jay Lerner Music Frederick Loewe, Chappell London

68 The Sound of Music, Piano selection, Music Richard Rodgers words Oscar Hammerstein

69 Joseph Amazing Technicolour Dreamcoat Music Andrew Lloyd Webber Words Tim Rice

70 Joseph Amazing Technicolour Dreamcoat – Novello – Sevenoaks, Kent

71 Phantom of the Opera – Music Andrew Lloyd Webber Words Charles Hart, extra sheets

72 The King and I, vocal score – Music Richard Rogers Words Oscar Hammerstein II

73 Something to sing – Geoffrey Brace, Cambridge Press, including 50 songs

74 Something to sing – Geoffrey Brace, Cambridge Press, edition 2 Another 50 songs

75 The Oxford School Music books Teacher's Manual Senior Part 1

76 The Oxford School Music books Teacher's Manual Senior Part II

As I wrote, at the start of this chapter, this list is just a small selection of the music that I rescued when allowing my vast collection to be given away. The room where the music was stored is now being used by myself and family. I am sure that people in other professions have similar problems to me.

Chapter 10

by Michael Parkinson

My Tribute to Iris

It has been a privilege working with Iris Broughton, who was 97 on 8 February 2025, to bring her story to you. Sadly she is suffering hearing loss and failing eyesight so she is not able to play piano or even read her music books now. In this chapter I have recommended some YouTube videos with songs and stories about Iris that I believe you will find interesting.

On 5 April 2001 Iris attended a concert performed by a piano quartet which I had promoted at the Djanogly Recital Hall on the campus of Nottingham University. During the first half, the pianist, Mitra Alice Tham played the famous Chaconne in D minor by J S Bach. After acknowledging applause Mitra walked back on stage and explained that she was going to play a composition based on a short theme provided by a member of the audience, she appealed for someone to provide the theme. At first no one volunteered but I heard someone say 'Come on Iris' and she stepped forward. The concert was filmed so whilst curating this book I obtained Mitra's permission to load the instant composition to YouTube so that you, the reader can see and hear what happened, Iris and Mitra can be seen with this title:-

Piano, instant composition for Iris by Mitra Alice Tham

The earliest video of Iris playing piano with the Netherfield singers was put on YouTube in 2010 by a man whose channel name is jimmyrior. In 2024, whilst I was curating this book, Jimmy gave permission for me to extract the choir segment and load it to my YouTube channel name 'Michael notthatone Parkinson'. This is the only video available of that choir performing with Iris at the piano. My YouTube title is:-

Netherfield Singers led by Iris Broughton, piano, Raindrops keep falling on my head

All the male members and most of the ladies dropped out of Netherfield singers so those that remained joined the Rose Singers. Iris was Musical Director

of them performing at the Methodist Church in Arnold on 5 November 2013.

I panned the camera round to obtain vision of Iris conducting from one minute to the end of this song, this was the first time I had videoed Iris on stage. The YouTube video title is:-

I Believe, Rose Singers, Methodist Church, Arnold, Nottingham 5 November 2013

I put seven titles on YouTube from that concert, here is the link to just one more of them:-

The Rose by the Rose Singers at Methodist Church Arnold, Nottingham on 5 Nov 2013

The following year Danielle Hall, a Radio and Television broadcaster joined the Rose Singers as Musical Director with Iris happily continuing as a choir member. The next concert was performed at the Mechanics Institute, Shakespeare Street, Nottingham. I loaded two songs to YouTube. The titles were:-

Snow Waltz, (Schneewalzer), Rose Singers, Nottingham 19 Dec 2014

White Christmas, Rose Singers, Mechanics Institute, Nottingham 19 Dec 2014

The Rose singers performed at the Netherfield and Colwick Senior Citizens Club where they sang two songs which are loaded to YouTube:-

Waiting at the Church, Maureen Shaw, Netherfield, Senior Citizens 6 Mar 2015

Iris insisted I must video the fun routine, she obviously has a good sense of humour.

The YouTube title is:-

Looking for a Man, Comedy Song, Rose Singers, 6 March 2015

My next date with the Rose singers was on 18 October 2016 at Carewatch situated on Woodborough Road in Nottingham. They had fun with their variation of Swing Low, When the Saints go Marching in and other songs. Musical Director Danielle Hall sang a solo. It was a pleasure to see the audience enjoying themselves. The YouTube title is:-

Rose Singers entertain at Carewatch, Nottingham 18 Oct 2016

The song that Danielle sang was separately loaded to YouTube with the title:-

Can't Help Loving That Man of Mine, Danielle Hall 18 Oct 2016

On St George's Day, 23 April 2017 the Rose Choir performed at the appropriately named St George's Church, Netherfield in Nottinghamshire. Iris can fleetingly be seen on the back row behind the second lady from the right. This selection of music includes songs from the Sound of Music, Gabriel Silver Trumpet, I'll Walk with God, Hallelujah and Rose of England. The YouTube title is:-

Rose Singers, Part 2, St George's Church Netherfield Nottingham 23 April 2017

On 15 May 2018 the Rose Singers were at United Reform Church in Bulwell, Nottingham, this time with Alec Jackson as Musical Director. He devised an arrangement of Teddy Bears Picnic which I liked. They added other songs in this medley and Iris is sometimes in vision on the right side of the second row. The YouTube title is:-

Teddy Bears Picnic, Oklahoma, Any Dream Will Do, Rose singers 15 May 2018

The last concert I videoed of Iris with the Rose singers was at St Mary's Church Arnold on 3 July 2023. They sang Can you feel the love tonight? I'll walk with God, The Lord is my Shepherd, (Vicar of Dibley), Wonderful World, Who knows where the time goes? I'd like to teach the world to sing, I enjoy being a girl, Sun in the morning, Diamonds are a girls best friend and Any Dream will do. Alec Jackson was The Musical Director with Geoff at the piano. The YouTube title is:-

Rose Singers, St Marys Church Arnold Nottingham 3 July 2020

Joan and I sometimes took Iris out for a meal to Mapperley Golf Club situated close to where she lives. On Friday 8 September 2023 the weather was beautiful so after we got back to her house we enjoyed sitting in the back garden. I got permission to video and put this on You Tube with the title:-

Iris Broughton talks about her son Neil who does the garden 8 Sep 2023

Neil does more than the garden, he does cleaning, washing, makes drinks and all sort of chores. He is a constant companion and with his cousin Paul they have taken Iris on holiday and transport her to various locations.

It has been an interesting but difficult task helping Iris to achieve her ambition of writing and publishing her story. She has been very patient in trying to answer my many questions and I have often had to ask Neil for help which he has willingly provided. The important thing is that we hope that you, the reader, have enjoyed reading it.

By the same author

Billy Fury to YouTube
ISBN 978-1-78222-588-1
Includes Billy Fury Dance Shows and biography, how Michael started on YouTube and his Thames Path Walk. The Blackpool Tower Ballroom to Scarborough Spa then Paris Disneyland adventure and the Thursford Christmas Spectacular story. Michael's childhood memories to National Service and biography complete his first book.

Ovaltineys to Sheredean Girls Club
ISBN 978-1-78222-675-8
A nostalgic story about girls growing up and making their own entertainment in the 1940s and 50s.

Early Years

Thames Path Walk
ISBN 978-1-78222-755-7
I walked all 184 miles of the Thames Path in 30 sections over 3 years. Every section was a single day outing starting from my home near Nottingham and travelling by train to, and back home, from London.

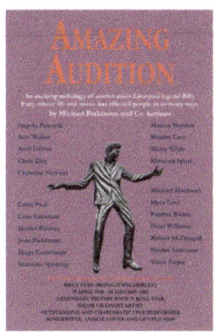

Amazing Audition
ISBN 978-1-78222-831-8
The Billy Fury Story by Michael and 22 Co-Authors includes 120 pictures